Catherwood remains an enigma to this day. First of all, we do not know what the man looked like: not a single picture of Catherwood exists today. William Brockedon, an artist who portrayed a great number of distinguished men at that time, ignored him completely and even his friends did not oblige us with a description of him. Secondly, it is almost impossible to discover any personal details about the man or his personality. Even his most intimate friends have not left us a line about his character, his interests or his good and bad points. He was the friend of great poets and artists but he was not referred to by any of them unless fleetingly. And yet Catherwood was an architect, an artist worthy of being a member of the Royal Academy and, above all, an archaeologist and explorer who made extraordinary discoveries. Even more disconcerting is the fact that of his enormous graphical, pictorial and cartographic output – hundreds of examples from views of Rome and Jerusalem to the ruins of ancient Egypt and classical Greece – only a fraction has survived, which deals almost exclusively with the Maya ruins of Central America. Much of this diverse material has been destroyed by accident, more has been lost for various reasons and who knows how much may still be hidden in the immense collections of the British Museum and never systematically studied. Modest to excess, Catherwood did very little to bring himself to public notice or to recognize the value of his work (which, objectively speaking, was of great documentary importance); however, it is also true that several of his contemporaries may have been able to benefit from his pathological reserve. For example, unscrupulous editors almost certainly published numerous views taken from Catherwood's works which he sold for little money or lent to deceitful engravers who left off his name. The academic world of the time, as we shall see when discussing James Fergusson, was at least in part responsible for this calamitous diaspora: for reasons of envy, for fear of new ideas or for obtuse partisanship to the then current theories. It is also to be expected that his drawings came into the hands of private collectors who would have had no desire to publicize their purchases.

What has remained, however, is enough to show incontrovertibly that Frederick Catherwood was an exceptional documenter and an extraordinary artist. He had a spirit in which the flame of curiosity, knowledge and culture burnt bright. Despite its limitations, this book is a tribute to one of the major figures of the 19th century who inexplicably remained in the shadow until recent times and whose splendid work is almost unknown to the general public.

Fabio Bourbon

Page 8-9 – Plate II, depicting the ruins of Copán, from the standard edition of *Views of Ancient Monuments in Central America, Chiapas and Yucatan*, by Frederick Catherwood.

THE BIRTH OF MR. CATHERWOOD

Frederick Catherwood – or "Mr. Catherwood" as even his best friends called him all his life – was born on 27 February 1799 in Charles Square, Hoxton, a suburb of London.

An aura of romantic mystery surrounds this most extraordinary person since it is not even known what he looked like. Even though it seems nearly impossible, no picture of Catherwood has survived that can give us the faintest idea of his appearance. Despite fame and being known by a great number of celebrated artists of the period, it seems no-one ever drew or painted his portrait or even paid him, or us, the courtesy of providing a description of the man, however brief. The only, authentic self-portrait that Catherwood executed was inserted in one of his canvasses (the Panorama of Jerusalem*) which has inauspiciously disappeared. John Lloyd Stephens, who was his intimate friend for fifteen years and who shared all types of adventure with him in the wilds of Central America, only speaks of him as "Mr. Catherwood" in his extensive diaries of their journeys together which were published in 1841 and 1843. Of Catherwood, there remains only this unusual epithet, so 18th century in its scrupulous formality, and a tiny figure that appears in a lithograph taken from his masterpiece,* Views of Ancient Monuments in Central America, Chiapas and Yucatan, *which has consigned his name and art to posterity. Catherwood is shown as a 40-year-old man of average build, with straight, long fair hair, wearing white trousers, a beige frock-coat and a crumpled white hat. In truth, much of the responsibility for the man's disconcerting anonymity is due to Frederick Catherwood himself, whose modesty could even have been pathological.*

The first symptoms of this extreme reserve became evident during his infancy but increased to excess as an adult. He was always cautious, rather formal, and tended to belittle himself. Often he would indulge in periods of complete silence or, to use a term that was beloved by doctors of the age, he fell subject to "bouts of melancholy". Nevertheless, he had an agile and brilliant intellect and was endowed with an inexhaustible enthusiasm and interior strength which were able to balance this pernicious form of depression and sustain him in difficult moments during his adventurous explorations of far-off lands. Nor do we know anything of his personality. A biography of Catherwood is therefore necessarily tied to mere objective data gathered from the few official documents and from the writings of those who knew him. These revolve essentially around his scholastic career, artistic experience and celebrated travels. What the passions were that moved his heart, what his tastes were, his qualities and faults, all these must remain relegated to the plan of pure inference.

Unfortunately, we do not even know about his family or his early years. Certainly his parents were well-off though they were not members of the aristocracy. His father, Nathaniel, had Scottish origins: the name Catherwood seems to be derived from a river near Edinburgh, the Calder. The family of his mother, Elizabeth, had an Irish background. Of Alfred, Frederick's only brother, born in 1803, it is only known that he graduated in medicine at the University of Glasgow, that he practised at the London Dispensary from 1842, that he published a treatise on pathologies of the lungs and that he died in 1865.

Pages 10-11 – In plate XXIV of *Views of Ancient Monuments in Central America, Chiapas and Yucatan* appears the only known image of Frederick Catherwood (to the right).

Page 22 left – Robert Hay (1799-1855) is shown dressed as a Turk in a daguerrotype.

Page 22, 23 – This view of the Nubian temple of Gerf Hussein was drawn by Catherwood in 1824 during his first trip down the Nile.

Page 23 top – The frontispiece of "Views in Cairo", published by Robert Hay in 1840.

years away. England was in that period undergoing great change and consequently social and economic tension. The Industrial Revolution was radically changing the country and against this difficult background, Catherwood tried to practise his profession as architect but with little luck. As usual, the information available on this period of his life is fragmentary and lacking in detail but it is known he designed several labourers' cottages and a large conservatory. No doubt he also had other commissions but not enough to support him. To put his finances back in order he sold some of the drawings he had made on the banks of the Nile and, feeling sure of the public's interest, he exhibited a number of illustrations at the Royal Academy, but even this initiative must have met with little success as, at the end of that year, he packed his bags in an instant and embarked once more for Egypt as soon as he received a letter from Robert Hay asking Frederick to join his expedition up the Nile.

After spending a few more days with Severn in Rome, Catherwood returned to Alexandria in 1829. It is a great misfortune that, with the exception of a few scribbled letters, this singular person did not leave any written description of his voyage which might be compared to those of other artists and explorers of the age. For example, ten years later, David Roberts described the huge city with evident emotion. "Alexandria was right in front of us, with mosques and palm-trees that gave it a different atmosphere from any I had ever breathed before . . . The bay was crowded with a large number of vessels, many of which were warships; our boat was soon surrounded by the most picturesque boatmen I have ever seen". Consequently, we are obliged to fill out Catherwood's conciseness with a little imagination of our own. The large port city was an indescribable confusion of sumptuously dressed gentlemen, naked black slaves, deafening camel drivers, Greek and Jewish merchants and people of every nationality that headed this way and that without any particular destination. Yet, notwithstanding the remains of its glorious past, greater interest was to be found in the streets of Cairo where the members of Robert Hay's group, who were studying the pyramids at Giza, met frequently. Catherwood's first task was to measure the dimensions and draw to scale the huge and eternal abodes of Cheops, Chephren and Mycerinus. The result of the expedition was forty nine large-folio

Page 24 – The temple of Wadi Sabua in Nubia drawn by Catherwood in 1824.

Pages 24, 25 – This splendid view of Abu Simbel in Nubia was also drawn by Catherwood during the 1824 expedition. Note that the entrance to the hypogeum rooms cleared of sand by Giovanni Battista Belzoni in 1817 was blocked once more.

volumes furnished with hundreds of pictures that Hay gave to the British Museum in 1879 where they are still kept. Strange though it may seem, Hay only found the time to publish one book during his lifetime, called Views in Cairo which was published in London in 1840. This volume contains just one of Catherwood's views of the Pyramids which consequently became one of the few works (with the exception of the illustrations of the Maya remains) that his contemporaries were able to admire. All the rest of his massive amount of documentation was either lost or is still kept in the Hay collection. About thirty years ago, the scholar Victor Wolfgang von Hagen managed to discover some of the original illustrations among the enormous quantity of paper and to attribute them correctly. This heavy task was made all the more burdensome by the fact that the reluctant "Mr Catherwood" had the terrible habit of not signing his drawings (or at most scribbling "FC" in the corner). Other sketches were later found in the same collection by other scholars but even today no definitive catalogue exists.

Frederick tackled his work with the same meticulousness and calligraphic precision of the ancient copyists but also shared with them the rule of silence and modesty. It is easy to imagine him sitting under the boiling sun completely absorbed in his work; a solitary and inscrutable figure even to his own companions. It is highly indicative that in the nearly five years that he and his colleagues were intent on their study of the Egyptian monuments, not a single word was written about his character. No witty remark or anecdote that

throws some light on his character has come down to us. The only fact we have is that he owned an extremely modern, seven round revolver (Colt only patented their first revolver in 1835) that greatly impressed the local people and was known throughout the Nile valley.

Once the expedition had finished studying the archaeological area of Giza, it moved camp to the ruins of Memphis. This used to be the capital of pharaonic Egypt during the Old Kingdom and is located near the sites of Sakkarah, Abusir, Meidum and Dashur. Here stand the famous Step Pyramid built by King Djoser, the Red Pyramid and the Rhomboidal Pyramid. When they had explored these monuments, the group moved south to Beni Hassan, Abydos and Dendera. By the end of summer 1832, Hay's expedition had arrived at the majestic ruins of ancient Thebes, the capital of Egypt during the Middle and New Kingdoms. The city of Thebes was located where the villages and temples of Luxor and Karnak now stand.

Catherwood spent September surveying the entire archaeological site and produced a detailed map with the ground plans of all the main buildings. He also drew the obelisks of the temple of Luxor, different views of the Ramesseum, and the interior of the tomb of Ramses IV with its enormous sarcophagus in the Valley of the Kings. Hay established the camp inside this sepulchre where it was cool and well-ventilated. Two views of the tomb of Sethi I, one of the tomb of Ramses III and a panorama of the entire valley can perhaps be ascribed to Catherwood. In the meantime, Arundale drew the two large sacred complexes of Karnak and Luxor and Bonomi reproduced as many hieroglyphics as possible plus wall paintings in the tombs so far discovered in the Valleys of the Kings and Queens.

In October, Catherwood accompanied another member of the expedition, George Hoskins, to the oasis of Kharga in the desert towards Libya. At the end of 1832, Frederick and James Haliburton began to measure and draw the Colossi of Memnon, the two immense statues erected by Amenhotep III in front of his own memorial temple of which only ruins now remain. To do so, he built scaffolding around them and measured every single element. His illustrations were the first to have been made with scientific accuracy and are still kept as part of the Hay collection. Catherwood made use of a "camera lucida" or light chamber to help him sketch the outline of an object on a piece of paper. The instrument had been invented some years before by William Wollaston and consisted of a four-sided prism on a stand over the drawing paper.

The expedition progressed south from Thebes stopping at Hermonthis, Esna, Edfu, Kom Ombo, Elephantine and, finally, on the wonderful island of Philae, just upstream of the First Cataract. In the weeks spent among the colonnades of the sanctuary consecrated to Isis, the untiring Catherwood continued to pile up an enormous amount of material, today mostly untraceable. Of all the illustrations

Page 27 – Portrait of Mohammed Ali, pasha of Egypt from 1805-49.

Page 41 – Count Jean Fréderic Waldeck (1766-1875) was an able artist but also an unscrupulous deceiver. In these two tables showing stucco panels at Palenque, the clothes and head-dresses (one has even been shown similar to an elephant) have been distorted to seem more classical in style.

Mexican artist Luciano Castañeda, who accompanied Captain Guillelmo Dupaix from 1805-07 in exploration of the ruins of Palenque and other sites, are a perfect example of how he and his colleagues did not understand what they were reproducing and that they were utterly incapable of faithfully bearing witness to a style they had never seen before.

Similarly, the missionaries, army officers, functionaries and adventurers that had written about the temples and objects buried in the forests in their accounts were not able to free themselves from their ethnocentrism and lack of imagination that rendered them irremediably blind to the evidence. No-one wanted to pay attention to names like Aztec, Mixtec, Toltec and Maya that had been passed down from the Conquistadors as being distinct peoples: the thinking was that all Indians were the descendants of the Jews that had come to the new world after the Flood. Few dared to put this sacrosanct "truth" in doubt. One of them was a colonel of the Guatemalan army that had published a book in 1835 called Descricción de las ruinas de Copán *that contained many drawings of the site and its buildings where he had carried out a rudimentary exploration and excavation the year before. Juan Galindo, too, must have had great intuition as he was the first to identify the hieroglyphic writing that he had seen at Copán and Palenque as being exclusive to the Mayan culture. It was Galindo's work, published in Paris in 1834 with the title* Antiquités Mexicaines, *that above all attracted the attention of Stephens and kindled his enthusiasm. Unlike his contemporaries, the lawyer was under the impression that at some remote time in the past, a magnificent civilisation had flourished in Central America, the art and archaeology of which needed to be studied on the spot. There was no lack of money as the income from his book* Incidents of Travel in Arabia Petrea, *in addition to that to come from* Incidents of Travel in Greece, Turkey, Russia and Poland, *published in 1838 by Harper Bros., were more than enough to finance an expedition. Three names were fixed in his mind, they were Copán, Palenque and Uxmal. These were the cities he was to search for in the jungles of Central America. Stephens was not the first to tread this path: in 1832, a French doctor named Corroy had written on one of the walls of the "Palace" at Palenque that he had been there three times – and accompanied by his wife and children – but he was certainly the first to try to interpret its secrets with objectivity.*

Once roused, Stephens was not a man to give in to obstacles. He began preparations and alerted Catherwood to his plans. Catherwood naturally volunteered to go with him without hesitation, which was exactly what the American needed: a trusted and experienced companion, unwavering when confronted by difficulties and, above all, an excellent artist. In a world where photography still did not exist (the Frenchman Louis-Jacques Daguerre had developed his first photographic plate in 1837 but it would be some years before pictures could be printed), artists played a fundamental role in scientific expeditions. It was they who provided

proof of and spread news of discoveries. Catherwood, who had spent much of his youth travelling in Egypt and Palestine, was fascinated by the descriptions of Palenque, the lost city in the jungle of Chiapas. Frederick had studied in depth the greatest architectural ruins around the Mediterranean and down the White Nile and he was sceptical of the theories that were currently in vogue. The buildings, sculptures and bas-reliefs that Stephens had shown him in the books sent him by Bartlett did not seem to have anything to do with the art of the Old World and, in particular, the drawings made by Waldeck seemed similarly suspect.

As the two firmed up their plans, chance lent a hand once more. In September 1839, the newly elected American chargé d'affaires in the Central American Federation suddenly died leaving the post vacant. Stephens, who had always been a Democrat, asked the Democrat President Van Buren if he could have the post. The New York lawyer was a well-known figure, though for his literary success rather than his political militancy, and had the backing of several influential people. However he got what he wanted and on 13 August he received an official letter which asked him to leave as soon as possible. His instructions were not clear, especially as the political situation in Central America was rather confused, but for Stephens this was a secondary detail. His position guaranteed him diplomatic immunity and that was what he needed. Once he had arrived at his destination, he could discharge his political duties as quickly as possible and then dedicate himself to searching for the lost cities of the Maya. In order to give himself an appearance fitting to his role, he had a blue uniform made up fitted with plenty of gold buttons. It was a gaudy dress uniform that, in its way, was to be extremely useful. On 9 September, Stephens and Catherwood – who had handed over management of the Panorama to his partner, Jackson – signed an agreement in which the first agreed to pay all the travel expenses and to guarantee payment of 1,500 dollars for the exclusive rights to use the graphical material produced on the trip.

of twenty five dollars per week to Mrs Catherwood and family during the absence of the said Catherwood; it being understood that all the money which shall be so paid to Mrs Catherwood and family shall be deducted from the aforesaid sum of $1500 or otherwise taken into the amount on a final settlement as so much money paid to the said Catherwood –

John L Stephens

New York September 9. 1839 F. Catherwood

Received two hundred dollars on account of the above sum of fifteen hundred. — F. C.

Catherwood agreed not to publish either drawings or accounts of his journey until Stephens gave his permission. After receiving 200 dollars on account, Frederick signed. Everything was ready, their greatest adventure was about to begin.

Pages 42, 43 – Waldeck has sneakily altered the shape of the mountain in this view of Palenque to make it look like a pyramid.

Page 42 – The drawing shows a bas-relief at Palenque. The Phrygian cap of the person on the throne, the cuneiform symbols and the Pan's pipe in the column of glyphs on the left are all the result of Waldeck's imagination.

Page 43 – This is the last page of the contract signed between Stephens and Catherwood on 9 September 1839.

THE MAYA REDISCOVERED

At this point of our story, a short digression about who the Maya were and the type of civilisation they created is appropriate. Questions regarding their civilisation are greatly answered by study of Catherwood's magnificent illustrations, published in 1844 after his two adventurous trips of exploration through the forests of Central America and across the plains of the Yucatán. For that reason, the tables which originally appeared with the title Views of Ancient Monuments in Central America, Chiapas and Yucatan, *even then considered his masterpiece, are published here.*

The twenty-six hand-coloured lithographs with his own descriptions are more illuminating and explicit than many learned discourses. Surprisingly detailed, they show without doubt that the Maya were the authors of some of the most artistic and intellectual works of pre-Columbian America. Besides large constructions, the Maya produced works of artistic refinement such as stone and plaster sculptures, frescoes, painted pottery and bas-reliefs in wood.

Developing out of the fertile culture created by the Olmecs (the people that spread across the Mexican highlands and along the Pacific coast as far as Guatemala during the 1st millennium BC), the Mayan civilisation reached its peak during the Classical Period between 250 – 950 AD. They controlled a huge area which covered what are today Guatemala and Belize and part of Honduras and El Salvador plus the Mexican regions of Chiapas and Tabasco. The Maya created centralised states guided by hereditary rulers often in conflict with each other. A flourishing economy based on intensive agriculture and trade of valuable goods such as jade, cocoa beans, obsidian, feathers and cotton encouraged rapid growth in the number of urban centres connected by an efficient road network. Their social organisation grew complex: at its head was the ruler who held political and military power and was responsible for the well-being of the community on a spiritual level. Society was rigidly divided by a hierarchy with priests and nobles at the top, then warriors, merchants, craftsmen, farmers and, at the bottom, slaves. Cities, some of which – such as Tikal, Copán, Palenque, Piedras Negras, El Mirador and many others – grew until they had populations of tens of thousands, they were built around monumental ceremonial centres, markets and large public buildings used for administration. Temples and palaces were built from stone; they were often plastered and

Page 45 – The frontespiece of *Views of Ancient Monuments* is by Owen Jones (1804-74), an architect and draughtsman who was actively interested in decorative problems.

IDOL AND ALTAR, AT COPÁN

In this Plate, the altar, or sacrificial stone, forms the principal object in the fore-ground. It is three feet six inches high, above the ground, and measures seven feet from angle to angle. It is sculptured into four hideous heads of colossal size, having enormous fangs, and distended eyes, adding, no doubt, the finishing horror to the bloody sacrifices which there can be little doubt were enacted on it. Certain channels (now nearly obliterated) exist on its upper surface, to carry off the blood of the human victim ; and to render the operation of cutting open the breast, and tearing out the heart more easy, the upper surface of the stone is slightly convex, agreeing with the accounts of the early Spanish discoverers. It was painted red, a fitting colour for so sanguinary a ritual. The Idol, to whom the sacrifice was offered, stands at a distance of twelve feet from the sacrificial stone. It is eleven feet nine inches high, and three feet square, cut out of a single block of stone, and has elaborate carvings on the back and sides. It is conjectured to be the portrait of some deified hero or chieftain, from certain traces of individuality in the features. There are remains of a beard and moustache, and the whole figure is enveloped and overladen with a complicated dress and head ornaments. It stands at the foot of a pyramidal terrace, or wall, which probably supported the sacred edifice.

The table shows what is now known as Stele D and its extraordinary altar which perhaps shows the god of death, Ah Puch. This monolith stands at the northern end of the Great Square, in front of the steps that lead to Temple 2. It is dated to 736 and is one of Copán's oldest altars.

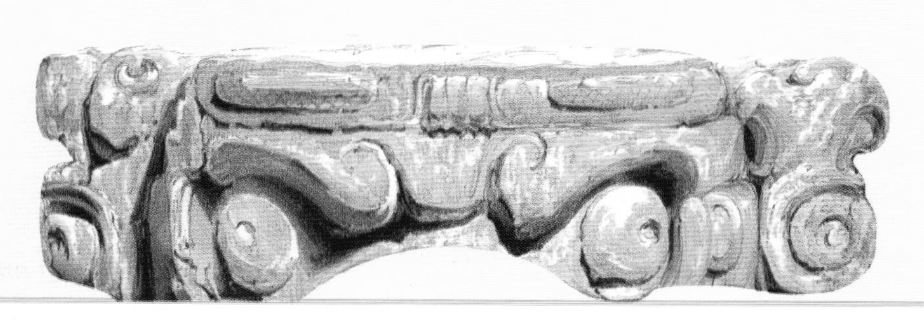

GENERAL VIEW OF PALENQUE

The ruins of Palenque are the first which awakened the attention to the existence of ancient and unknown cities in America.

They lie twelve miles distant, in a south-easterly direction from Palenque, the last village northward in the State of Chiapas. They have no other name than that of the village near which they are situated, but in the neighbourhood they are called "Las Casas de Piedra," or, "the Houses of Stone."

The extent of the ruin is not very great, at least, so far as we were able to survey; and we visited all the buildings mentioned by Del Rio and Dupaix. A square space, one thousand yards each way, would include them all; but the extent of ground is apparently much larger, which deception, no doubt, arises from the difficulty and time required to pass from one spot to another, from the extreme denseness of the tropical vegetation.

The largest and most important structure is called the Palace, seen to the left in the drawing. The principal front faces the east, and is the opposite one to that shown by the drawing. It measures two hundred and twenty-eight feet, and the same on the rear. The two side-fronts each measure one hundred and eighty feet. Its height does not exceed twenty-five feet, and all around it had a bold projecting cornice of stone. It stands on an artificial mound, forty feet high, three hundred and ten feet front and rear, and two hundred and sixty feet on each side. These are its principal dimensions. The front and rear had each fourteen doorways, and the ends, eleven. The openings are about nine feet wide, and the piers between six and seven feet. The entire building was of stone, stuccoed and painted, with spirited bas reliefs on the piers, and projecting borders of hieroglyphics, and other ornaments. It had three principal court-yards, the largest of which is given in the following Plate. There are several interesting portions of stone sculpture, and of paintings in colours, connected with this building; the latter, especially, is being fast obliterated by the excessive dampness prevailing the greater part of the year. The vegetation, at the time of our visit, was close and rank, and it was not without considerable labour, in the cutting away of trees, that the entire design of the building could be made out.

In the fore-ground of the drawing is seen an elevated pyramidal mound, which appears once to have had steps on all its sides. These steps have been thrown down by the growth of trees, making the ascent very difficult. The mound, measured on the slope, is one hundred and ten feet. On the platform, at top, is a stone Casa, or House, seventy-six feet in front, and twenty-five feet deep. It has doors and piers still standing, the end piers being ornamented with hieroglyphics, and the centre ones with figures. The interior of the building

is divided into two corridors, running lengthways, with ceilings formed of over-lapping stones, rising nearly to a point, and floors paved with large square stones. The corridors are each seven feet wide, separated by a massive wall, and the back one divided into three chambers. The centre room contains a stone tablet of hieroglyphics, and there are two others in the front corridor. The roof is inclined, and the sides are covered with stucco ornaments, now much broken, but enough remains to show that it must, when perfect, have been rich and imposing. On the top was a range of small square piers, covered by a layer of flat projecting stones, which gives it the appearance of a low open balustrade.

The two Casas in the distance, and to the right of the high mound, are very similar in construction to the one just described. They were richly ornamented both with sculpture and painting, as also with works in stucco. Each stands on its respective mound, with stone staircases, now overgrown with trees and shrubs. There are two other Casas of smaller dimensions, but so much ruined that little more than their outline remains.

The high hill, in the back-ground of the picture, appeared so regular that, but for its great height (nearly one thousand feet), we should have supposed it artificial. On the summit are the remains of an ancient structure.

It is due to the reader to state, that this general view of Palenque is composed of separate sketches of each Casa, or Building, and from the ground-plan each is made to occupy its respective position. No other method could be adopted, as the large size of the trees, and dense nature of the forest, precluded any idea of making a clearing sufficient to embrace them all in one view. The clearing is, therefore, not real, but imaginary. The remainder of the drawing may be considered as quite faithful..

Palenque was in fact much larger than Catherwood thought. The site stretches on three different levels for a little over 2 miles from east to west and for more than half a mile north to south. Only a small part has so far been systematically explored and restored. The "pyramidal tumulus" described by Catherwood is today known as the Pyramid of the Inscriptions due to the hieroglyphic texts inside the temple on the top of the structure. The "balustrade" is all that remains of the tall perforated crest that crowned the temple and that was typical of sacred Mayan buildings in Chiapas and Campeche. It should also be noted, despite what the author says, that the illustration is not exact as the mountain is actually directly behind the pyramid: this is an example of Romantic "poetic licence" which Catherwood took to make the view more attractive.

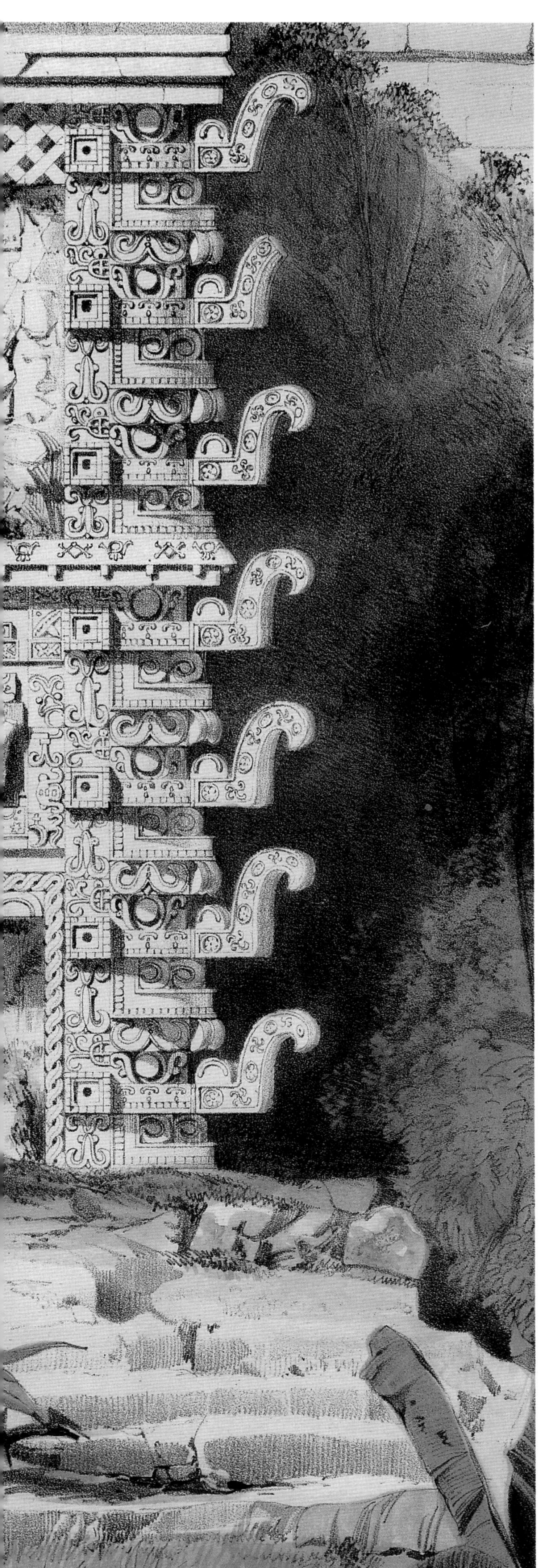

GATEWAY OF THE GREAT TEOCALLIS, UXMAL

The great Teocallis at Uxmal is called, by the Indians, the "House of the Diviner;" and also the "Dwarf's House." It is a lofty pyramidal mound, about two hundred and thirty-five feet long, by a breadth of one hundred and fifty-five feet. Its height is eighty-eight feet, and to the top of the building, one hundred and five feet. At the height of sixty feet is a solid projecting platform, formerly reached by a steep flight of steps, now thrown down. On this platform stands the gateway represented in the drawing. It measures twenty-two feet in front, and is twenty-two feet high, and was most elaborately adorned with sculptured stone-work. The ornaments are of similar design to those of the Casa del Gobernador, but executed perhaps with a greater degree of delicacy. The remains of two statues are seen, and most likely the niche in the centre was for the reception of a larger one. The doorway is five feet five inches wide, and ten feet high, with lintels of sapote wood still in their places. The interior is divided into two apartments, the outer, fifteen feet long, by seven feet wide, and nineteen feet high; and the inner one, twelve feet long, four feet wide, and eleven feet high. Both are entirely destitute of ornament, and it is not easy to conjecture to what end they served, as they are small, and have no apparent connection with the rest of the building.

The table reproduces the west temple of the Pyramid of the Magician (which Catherwood called "house") built during the fourth phase of the expansion of the structure. It is decorated in Chenes style (earlier than Puuc) with the entrance in the form of a serpent's jaws encircled by two rows of masks of the god Chac.

ORNAMENT OVER THE GATEWAY OF THE GREAT TEOCALLIS, UXMAL

This elegant specimen of Indian design and workmanship forms part of the front of the upper building of the Diviner's House, mentioned in the preceding description. The edifice is seventy-two feet in length and twelve feet deep. The interior is divided into three apartments, the centre one twenty-four by seven, and the side ones nineteen by seven. These apartments did not communicate with each other; the side ones had each a doorway opening to the eastward, and the middle room a doorway facing the west now destroyed of which the position is shown in the drawing. The ornament is somewhat different in character to that of the other buildings at Uxmal. The relief is low, and, unassisted by bright colours, would hardly have been visible from the ground, even aided by the transparent atmosphere of a tropical climate. There can be little doubt (speaking by analogy) that the entire facade was painted, although all traces of colour have disappeared. The pedestals and remains of eight statues are visible on this facade.

The temple on the summit was part of the last expansion of the Pyramid of the Magician; it was built in Puuc style and has two facades. The side facing east can only be reached by a steep stairway while the side facing west (shown) has two smaller sets of steps which frame the Chenes-style temple seen in the preceding table and reach its terrace.

PLATE XIII

GENERAL VIEW OF UXMAL, TAKEN FROM THE ARCHWAY OF LAS MONJAS, LOOKING SOUTH

This view embraces several of the most remarkable ruins at Uxmal, and the remaining ones are shown by Plate VIII. To the extreme left, in the distance, is the "Casa de la Vieja", or of the "Old Woman", a small teocallis, having at its base the rudely sculptured statue of a woman, from which it derives its name. The second and most colossal terrace of the Casa del Gobernador is seen extending to the right; and in the centre of the view is the casa itself, seen endwise: for a description of it, see Plate IX. Beneath it, and a little to the right, is the "Casa de las Tortugas," or "House of the Turtles:" this name was given to it by Padre Carillo, of Ticul, from a bead, or row, of turtles, which goes entirely round the building on the upper cornice. The length of this edifice is ninety-four feet by a depth of thirty-four, and, in size and ornament, contrasts strikingly with the Casa del Gobernador. It wants the rich and gorgeous decoration of the former, but is distinguished for its justness and beauty of proportion, and its chasteness and simplicity of ornament: unhappily it is fast going to decay. In 1839, it was trembling and tottering, and by 1842, the whole of the centre had fallen in, and the interior was blocked up with the ruins of the fallen roof. Beyond the Casa de las Tortugas are two large teocalli, on the nearest of which are no remains of building, but the furthest has on its summit the ruins of an edifice, somewhat similar in its plan to the structure of the Great Teocallis, or "House of the Diviner". In front of the last building stands the "Casa de Palomos", or "House of the Pigeons": it is two hundred and forty feet long, composed of a double range of rooms, from the dividing wall of which rise pyramidal structures, not unlike the gables of an Elizabethan or Gothic house. The small oblong openings give them somewhat the appearance of pigeon houses, whence the name.

As usual, Catherwood's description is more than exhaustive. We can only add that the two *monticoli* in the foreground were all that remained of the ball-court – an important structure in any Mayan city – and that the "triangular walls", today known as "combs", were a typical decorative element of Mayan architecture. The function of the building is still open to conjecture.

Well at Bolonchen

Bolonchen derives its name from two Maya words, Bolon, which signifies "nine," and Chen, "wells;" and it means "the nine wells." From time immemorial, nine wells formed at this place the centre of a population, and these are now in the plaza of the village. Their origin is as obscure and unknown as that of the ruined cities which strew the land, and as little thought of.

The custody and supply of these wells form a principal part of the business of the village authorities, but with all their care the supply of water lasts but seven or eight months in the year. At the period of our visit the time was approaching when the wells would fail, and the inhabitants be driven to an extraordinary cavern, at half a league's distance from the village.

There was one grand difficulty in the way of our visiting the cavern, or well. Since the commencement of the rainy season it had not been used; and every year, before having recourse to it, there was a work of several days to be done in repairing the ladders.

Setting out, however, from the village of Bolonchen, by the Campeachy road, we turned off by a well beaten path, following which we fell into a winding lane, and, descending gradually, reached the foot of the rude, lofty, and abrupt opening, under a bold ledge of overhanging rock, seeming a magnificent entrance to a great temple for the worship of the God of nature.

We disencumbered ourselves of superfluous apparel, and following the Indians, each with a torch in his hand, entered a wild cavern, which, as we advanced, became darker. At the distance of sixty paces the descent was precipitous, and we went down by a ladder about twenty feet. Here all light from the mouth of the cavern was lost, but we soon reached the brink of a great perpendicular descent, to the very bottom of which a strong body of light was thrown from a hole in the surface; a perpendicular depth, as we afterwards found by measurement, of two hundred and ten feet. As we stood on the brink of this precipice, under the shelving of an immense mass of rock, seeming darker from the stream of light thrown down the hole, gigantic stalactites and huge blocks of stones assumed all manner of fantastic shapes, and seemed like monstrous animals or deities of a subterraneous world.

From the brink on which we stood, an enormous ladder of the rudest possible construction led to the bottom of the hole. It was between seventy and eight feet long, and about twelve feet wide, made of the rough trunks of saplings lashed together lengthways, and supported all the way down by horizontal trunks braced against the face of the precipitous rock. The ladder was double, having two sets, or flights, of rounds, divided by a middle partition, and the whole fabric was lashed together by withes. It was very steep, seemed precarious and insecure, and confirmed the worst accounts we had heard of the descent into this extraordinary well.

Our Indians began the descent, but the foremost had hardly got his head below the surface, before one of the rounds broke, and he only saved himself by clinging to another. The ladder having been made when the withes were green, there were now dry, cracked, and some of them broken. We attempted a descent with some little misgivings; but by keeping each hand and foot on a different round, with an occasional crash and slide, we all reached the foot of the ladder; that is, our own party, our Indians, and some three or four of our escort, the rest having disappeared. Plate XX. represents the scene at the foot of this ladder. Looking up, the view of its broken sides, with the light thrown down from the orifice above, was the wildest that can be conceived. As yet we were only at the mouth of this well, called by the Indians, "La Senora escondida;" or, "the Lady hidden away:" and it is derived from a fanciful Indian story, that a lady, stolen from her mother, was concealed by her lover in this cave. On one side of the cavern is an opening in the rock, entering by which, we soon came to an abrupt descent, down which was another long and trying ladder. It was laid against the broken face of the rock, not so steep as the first, but in a much more rickety condition: the rounds were loose, and the upper ones gave way on the first attempt to descend. The cave was damp, and the rock and the ladder were wet and slippery. It was evident that the labour of exploring this cave was to be greatly increased by the state of the ladders, and there might be some danger attending it; but, even after all we had seen of caves, there was something so wild and grand in this that we could not bring ourselves to give up the attempt. Fortunately, the Cura had taken care to provide us with a rope, and fastening one end round a large stone, an Indian carried the other down to the foot of the ladder. We followed one at a time; holding the rope with one hand, and with other grasping the side of the ladder: it was impossible to carry a torch, and we were obliged to feel our way in the dark, or with only such light as could reach us from the torches above and below. At the foot of this ladder was a large cavernous chamber, with irregular passages branching off in different directions to seven deposite or sources of water, from which the village of Bolonchen is supplied.

Las Monjas, Chichén Itzá

The plate represents the end facade of a long majestic pile, called, like one of the principal buildings at Uxmal, the "Monjas," or "Nuns." The height of this facade is twenty-five feet, and its width thirty-five. It has two cornices of tasteful design; over the doorway are twenty small cartouches of hieroglyphics, in four rows, five in a row, and to make room for which the lower cornice is carried up; over them stand out, in a line, six bold projecting curved ornaments, resembling an elephant's trunk; and the upper centre space over the doorway is an irregular circular niche, in which portions of a seated figure, with a head-dress of feathers, still remain. The rest of the ornaments are of that distinctive stamp, characteristic of the ancient American cities, and unlike the designs of any other people. The building is composed of two structures, entirely different from each other; one of which forms a sort of wing to the principal edifice, and has at the end the facade presented. The whole length is two hundred and twenty-eight feet, and the depth of the principal structure is one hundred and twelve feet. The only portion containing interior chambers is that which we have called the wing. The great structure to which the wing adjoins is apparently a solid mass of masonry, erected only to hold up the two ranges of buildings upon it. A grand staircase, fifty-six feet wide, the largest we saw in the country, runs to the top. This staircase is thirty-two feet high, and has thirty-nine steps. On the top of the structure stands a range of buildings, with a platform of fourteen feet in front, extending all around. From the back of this platform the grand staircase rises again, by fifteen steps, to the roof of the second range, which forms a platform in front of the third range. The circumference of this building is six hundred and thirty-eight feet, and its height, when entire, was sixty-five feet. The art and skill of the builders seem to have been lavishly expended upon the second range: this is one hundred and four feet long and thirty feet wide; and the broad platform around it, though overgrown with grass several feet high, formed a noble promenade, commanding a magnificent view of the whole surrounding country.

Chichén Itzá was a large centre that flourished between the 9th and 10th centuries AD. It contains some of the most elegant Mayan monuments. The Nunnery, so called by its discoverers for its resemblance to a convent, is a masterpiece of Puuc art. The abundance of decoration does not hide the functional purity of the architectural lines (as, for example, at Kabah) giving a pleasing impression overall. What Catherwood called "hieroglyphs" are know by modern archaeology as glyphs – the characters of Mayan writing – which have mostly been deciphered in recent years. It is obvious that the English artist had understood the real nature of the signs which many of his contemporaries had considered as simple ornamental elements.

Catherwood left the miserable city accompanied by a French servant named Augustin whose face had been slashed by a machete and who was diabolically cunning. Their means of transport was a paddle steamer, the Vera Paz: they headed south down the Rio Dulce from where they reached Lake Yzabal. Although tortuous, this was an obligatory route as there were no other means of communication between the coast and the inland. The surrounding forest seemed particularly quiet and the only creatures they saw were pelicans, probably disturbed by the noise of the steamer's boilers which Stephens hated with all his heart. Both had travelled far and wide but neither had ever seen such luxuriant vegetation before. In the village of Yzabal where the steamer finally stopped, they had their first direct experience with the insalubrity of the region when the English engineer of the Vera Cruz fell ill with malaria. Catherwood certainly had no idea he would one day suffer the same misfortune. Stephens, meanwhile, had visited the grave of his compatriot, James Shannon, also American chargé d'affaires to Central America, who had died some years before in this godforsaken place. The tomb was squalid and poor Stephens was forced to ponder that three other of his predecessors had fallen to the same fate far from home.

The path that led over Mount Mico and into the heart of the jungle left from the small village on the shores of the crystal clear lake. Stephens, Catherwood and Augustin loaded their victuals and equipment onto mules and headed off towards the unknown with four Indian escorts. There was little to be cheerful about. Guatemala, the borders of which they were about to cross, was in the hands of Carrera, an Indian that was conducting a no holds barred war against Morazan, the white ruler of Salvador, and the mulatto Ferrera, ruler of Honduras. These latter two had only recently met in battle near San Salvador and now Morazan was moving against Guatemala with his bands of bloodthirsty cut-throats. Don Juan Peñol, the commander of the port of Yzabal, had warned Stephens not to place any reliance on his diplomatic immunity and added that the pass he had just been given would have little value if they came into contact with Morazan's men. It is evident that the two explorers wished to reach Copán in the shortest time possible as the Mayan city was not situated in the theatre of operations.

Armed with a pistol and a sword, Augustin headed the party along an increasingly muddy and steep path. To make progress even more difficult, they had to cope with the deep shade produced by the thick vegetation overhead, the enormous tree roots and the holes in the ground filled with water from the storms of the last few days. In short, no-one had much to say and the group fell into a profound silence. The mules tripped and fell continuously, the insects gave them no peace and the mud had transformed them into grotesque parodies of mounts and riders. The jungle, overarched by gigantic mahogany trees, got even thicker; it was a surreal universe consisting of dripping leaves, extraordinary flowers, enormous butterflies, tree toads and snakes that would undoubtedly have fascinated a biologist but not two travellers wanting only to shine light onto ancient civilisations.

Depressed by Shannon's grave, Stephens thought that their epitaph would sound inglorious: "Tossed over the head of a mule, brained by the trunk of a mahogany tree, and buried in the mud of the Mico Mountains".

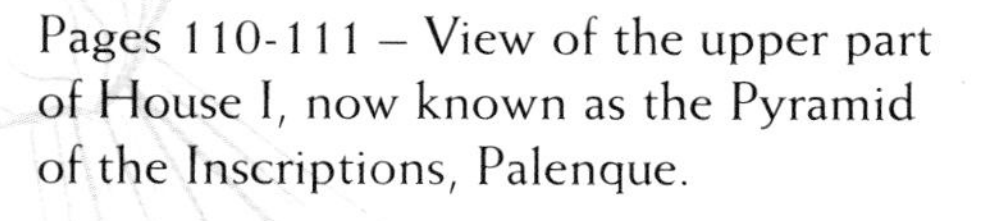

Pages 110-111 – View of the upper part of House I, now known as the Pyramid of the Inscriptions, Palenque.

Page 111 – Stucco bas-relief, Palenque

Page 112 – Stela P (623 AD) seen from the front, Copán.

A little later and quite unexpectedly, Catherwood was thrown out of the saddle with such force that his companion was petrified with horror for some seconds, convinced Catherwood was dead. As this was not the case, however when Frederick recovered from the blow, he gave Stephens a tongue lashing saying that if he had ever known of this mountain beforehand, Stephens would have had to come to Central America alone. For once, Frederick had lost his aplomb. A moment later and Augustin was thrown to the ground.

In the middle of this daylight nightmare, the group came across a rather absurd figure. Tall, dressed in a muddy poncho and wearing a wide-brimmed Panama hat, he brandished an enormous machete in his right hand and huge spurs jangled on his boots. The apparition bowed and, in perfect English that left them astonished, explained that he was a British gentleman coming from Nueva Guatemala where he had been a bank manager for the past two years and that now he was trying to return home with a bagful of shares. In the presence of such a figure, Catherwood and Stephens must have thought they were not the only madmen in that region after all.

On the second day, the group finally exited the forest and entered an area of highlands surrounded by snow-capped mountains and dotted with gigantic cactuses and mimosa bushes. The march continued through the villages of El Pozo, Enquentros and Gualan that were no more than a handful of adobe houses with straw roofs. Stephens' diplomatic mission was to track down any government in Central America, for which purpose he first had to head directly for

Page 113 – Fragment of sculpture, acropolis of Copán.

Nueva Guatemala. Nonetheless, his plans were slightly different and first he intended to visit the ruins of Copán that he had read so much about in the accounts of Juan Galindo and Domingo Juarros.

They travelled through the valley of the river Motagua as far as Zacapa where they turned south towards Chiquimula situated in the middle of corn fields, banana plantations and rows of prickly pear cactus plants. The local people were friendly and offered their hospitality so that Catherwood and Stephens never had to suffer hunger despite losing many of their provisions when they were accidentally mixed with gunpowder. The diet of tortillas and beans, though, was rather monotonous. The only real discomfort was the sun but even this provided an attraction, though somewhat embarrassing for two gentlemen: to cope with the heat, the clothes of the local women were rather scanty and it is easy to imagine how wide Stephens' and Catherwood's eyes must have opened in admiration. The pages of the American's diary contained many appreciations of the raven-haired young girls they met on the roads though he never managed to accept the passion they had for cigars. All went well until they entered the tiny village of Comatán which was no more than a bunch of small houses around a church with the usual dazzling white plastered facade. Here they were taken prisoner by a group of armed bandits – Indians, whites and mestizos – who took their orders from a young "officer" in the pay of General Cascara, one of General Carrera's allies. He wanted to see the personal documents of the two foreigners but he understood so little that he decided to ask for instructions from his superior. The General was at that moment in Chiquimula and the group would therefore have had to remain holed up in their hovel for an unknown period. Stephens flew into a temper but this achieved nothing, so Catherwood decided to intervene with all his British phlegm, treating his amazed audience to a dignified lecture on "the law of nations, the right of an ambassador, and the danger of bringing down upon them the vengeance of the government del Norte". But even this eloquent speech did not untangle the situation which was only resolved a day later with the arrival of an older officer who allowed the two to send a letter to Cascara. Stephens dictated the text and Frederick translated it into Italian – the General's mother tongue – signing it as the "secretary" of the American ambassador. In place of an official stamp, the wax was sealed with a new half dollar. Several hours later, they were finally allowed to proceed.

Finally at Copán

Once they had left this ugly episode behind them, Stephens and Catherwood had to march for two more days, cross the Copán river several times and climb a few hills before reaching their longed for destination on 13 November. Their troubles, though, were not ended. The village of Copán was no more than "half a dozen miserable huts" and the hacienda of Don Gregorio, a man they found impossible to deal with. Irate, vulgar, coarse and ignorant of the most basic elements of hospitality, this cantankerous person with a coal black moustache was, unfortunately, one of the most powerful people in the area and he was not at all keen on the foreigners. Not only did he not like their appearance, he disliked the Italian accent Catherwood used when he spoke Spanish, nor was he keen on being spoken to in French by Augustin. Since these characters who had appeared from nowhere were more than likely spies, Don Gregorio refused to give them any information on the ruins or let his men help them, even as a guide. With this fresh wave of hostility, and offended by the manner in which they were treated, Stephens was ready to explode but once again his quiet assistant intervened. In the book Incidents of Travel, Stephens describes and mentions his companion infrequently but, although taciturn, Catherwood must have been a good travel companion. From the few notes on the subject, a figure, with a certain character, emerges as well as an excellent practical sense that was able to temper the angry outbursts of the American and reason with him. In this difficult situation with Don Gregorio too, Frederick succeeded in calming Stephens and suggested greater diplomacy. This must have had the desired effect as Don Gregorio, perhaps scared of attracting the ire of the pair's mysterious allies, disappeared the next day and one of his sons found them a guide named José. In a short time, José cut a path through the jungle with his machete to the river Copán and on the other side they saw "a stone wall, perhaps a hundred feet high, with furze growing out of the top, running north and south along the river". Stephens did not realise the nature of the ruin, which was in fact a section of the Acropolis undermined by the river, and believed it was a wall to protect the city. Anyway, he understood he had entered on virgin territory and that he was close to opening a new chapter in the study of American civilisations. He was right. That moment was of supreme importance, not only for the knowledge of Copán, but of the entire Mayan civilisation.

José found a ford where they crossed the river. Hacking with his machete, he led them through the massive ruins buried beneath the luxuriant vegetation. The only

dangerous since bands of guerrillas, disbanded soldiers and common criminals ran riot in villages, killing and terrorizing whoever opposed them. Stephens was disconcerted because the capital had seemed so very beautiful to him, imbued with that romanticism that was peculiar to Spanish cities, with low houses rendered with lime and perfumed plants climbing around the windows. The idyllic appearance was hard to reconcile with the bloody atmosphere that reigned. Once he had taken possession of the building for the American delegation, he decided to follow the diplomatic instructions he had received. He began searching for the Guatemalan government and its representatives, but in vain. Francisco Morazan was in an all-out struggle with Rafael Carrera and the democratic institutions were nothing but a memory. Just then, no-one could have said who represented the political interests of Guatemala or the whole of Central America. By the end of December, it was clear to Stephens that if ever there had been a semblance of government in Guatemala, it certainly was there no longer. In the meantime, he had met in person the feared and victorious General Carrera who had struck him by his strong personality, but he had been of no help. The only thing Stephens could do was to pack up the documents left in the offices of the embassy and ship them back to the United States. Then, having dispensed with his political duties, he decided to permit himself a little tourism: he visited the ruins of Antigua Guatemala, climbed to the top of the Agua volcano, reached the Pacific coast and passed through a myriad of villages. He indulged his curiosity everywhere he went and he spent most of his time up till Christmas walking in the mountains or wandering through local market places.

Meanwhile, camped in the ruins of Copán, Catherwood was fighting two personal battles: one to master the redundant and complex art of the Maya in full, the other to defend himself from the mosquitoes. He won the first battle but lost the second. After three weeks spent in the forest, he succumbed to the malaria meted out by the anopheles mosquito. Laid prostrate by the fever, he was also robbed of food, blankets and other materials by one of the mule-drivers. In his suffering, he was forced to knock at the door of Don Gregorio who, to his enormous surprise, welcomed him in and attempted to alleviate the fever (evidently, it was the American who roused the anger of the grumpy old man). As soon as he got better, Frederick wrote to Stephens to explain the situation and decided to follow on in the shortest time possible.

Page 126 – A hut in the midst of a clearing planted with tobacco and maize, Copán. Stephens and Catherwood lived in a similar structure.

Pages 126-127 – The main square of Antigua Guatemala.

During his trip, while he was still on the Motagua river, he learned of another group of ruins hidden in the forest about 28 miles north of Copán and, although he was still weak, he could not resist the temptation to visit them. So it was that he discovered the remains of Quiriguá, today famous for the enormous stelae sculpted out of red sandstone, the largest so far found on Mayan territory.

The city was probably founded around 450 and abandoned shortly after 810. It is similar to Copán in its layout. The ruins of the main group stand around a great rectangular square dotted with stelae and running north-south. The Acropolis stands on the southern side. It was thought that Quiriguá was a colony of Copán for a long time but in 1978 this hypothesis was finally disproved. It seems instead that the two centres were reciprocally hostile: many local monuments show the capture of the ruler of Copán, Rabbit 18 (this is how the hieroglyphics that tell us his name are read in the absence of a better interpretation), in 737 during the reign of the 14th king of Quiriguá. Regardless of their political vicissitudes, the local architecture and art are clearly dependent on those of nearby Copán and Catherwood immediately understood that. The only difference was that the reliefs on the stelae appeared less accentuated besides being less dynamic in their designs.

Unfortunately, Quiriguá stands in the middle of a wet tropical forest and its more hostile climate than that of Copán meant that Frederick had to follow a fast-flowing river and then cut through a mile of jungle with his machete to reach the site, a task "such as none can fully understand who have not been in a

tropical country". This obviously was not the place for someone recovering from malaria and Frederick only spent enough time there to draw the two best preserved stelae, now identified as E and F.

On Christmas Day, a worn out, pale, thin and armed to the teeth "Mr Catherwood" finally made his entrance to Nueva Guatemala. Stephens welcomed him with great relief, especially as he was preparing to leave on his research. They celebrated New Year and then Stephens wanted to restart his political mission: if there was no government in Guatemala, then he had to look for one in Salvador or one of the other neighbouring countries, but this journey too turned into a nightmare as Stephens also fell prey to malaria. Luckily, Catherwood was with him which was a bonus even if only because the Englishman had had some experience of the subject. "Not having killed any one at Copán, he had conceived a great opinion of his medical skill" and it was Frederick who administered the doses of quinine, making sure they hit the mark. In addition to everything else, Frederick was a precise and well-organised man so that for a few days he saw to the food and all other practical contingencies. Once they reached the Pacific coast, Stephens went on by boat towards Salvador while Catherwood returned to Copán where he thought he had left too much work unfinished. Once more Don Gregorio, transformed from a gruff and cantankerous old codger into a gentleman, offered him warm hospitality and the Englishman was able to return to his pencils.

While the one continued his archaeological exploration, the other crossed the length and breadth of Salvador, Costa Rica and Nicaragua, passing from one theatre of war to another. After countless vicissitudes, innumerable miles through the forests, strong doses of quinine to hold off recurrent fever, spectacular volcanic landscapes, picturesque villages, gold mines and coffee plantations, Stephens was finally able to return to Nueva Guatemala, richer in experience but having seen neither hide nor hair of a government.

It was the end of March 1840 and at that point the "Mr. Minister of the United States" decided that it was the moment to tender his resignation and hurry off to the ruins of Palenque in the Mexican state of Chiapas as the rainy season would soon begin.

Page 128 top – The expedition progresses with difficulty through the forest. Stephens, exhausted, is carried on the back of a bearer.

Page 128 – Fragment of sculpture, acropolis area, Copán.

Page 129 – Colossal stela, Quiriguá.

Carrera had by now finally defeated Morazan and just installed himself in Guatemala City but he could not by any means be considered a reliable politician. So Stephens wrote a letter to Washington explaining the situation and stating that, given the circumstances, he considered further stay in the country completely unjustified. Finally, Catherwood (after spending a month in a monastery in Antigua to get his health back) knocked once again at the door of the American delegation one evening and the two embraced promising solemnly not to separate again while in such a dangerous place. In early April, the new expedition was ready but before leaving Stephens presented himself to General Carrera to ask for a pass to enable them safe conduct during the difficult journey to Palenque. This Carrera provided with ostentatious pride. The march was of course similar, if not more difficult, than that from Belize to Copán with the jungle throwing up all the obstacles it had at its disposal – mud, rain, creepers, roots, insects and poisonous plants besides the occasional earth tremor. The path grew more laborious as they neared the agave covered highlands of Guatemala and the hostile forests of Petén. The two found the time to stop briefly to explore the remains of Utatlán near Santa Cruz del Quiché, and another Mayan site named Toniná near to Ocosingo in Guatemala, but the two sites were so ruined that Catherwood had little to draw. Near Santa Cruz, the two bumped into a very strange person who turned out to be the priest of the village. He was a cultivated man from Spain who looked upon the world with ferocious irony and knew many

Page 131 centre – View of the ruins of Utatlán.

Page 131 bottom – View and plan of a pyramid-shaped religious building, Utatlán.

stories about the ancient Maya. Among other things, he told them of a mysterious city that was still populated by descendants of the powerful lords who had built it centuries before. It had white "towers" that poked out over the tops of green trees and was located just four days march away. Although Stephens and Catherwood were tempted, they decided that the time they had available was too limited and with heavy hearts they soldiered on. If instead they had followed the direction of the unusual Dominican priest, they would have found the remains of Tikál, one of the largest and most spectacular Maya cities.

After stopping at Quetzaltenango, a charming city that pleased the artistic tastes of Catherwood, they reached Huehuetenango near the border with Mexico where they were shown several ancient ruins. Here they met an American, John Pawling, who had already met Stephens some weeks before at Amatitlán. Tired of the war engulfing Guatemala, Pawling asked to join their expedition, an "honour" that was quickly accorded him. The last days of the journey were spent in a jungle lashed by rain and divided by fast running rivers and gorges hundreds of feet deep. It was a torment.

Pages 130-131 – Map of the ruins of Santa Cruz del Quiché, the ancient Maya site of Utatlán.

Page 130 bottom – View of a pyramid-shaped religious building in Utatlán.

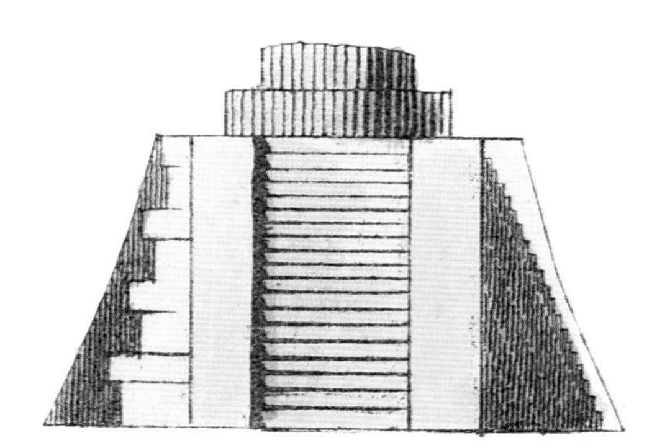

F. Catherwood

A.L. Dick.

On the fourth of June, they left Palenque forever, "like rats that abandon the ship after the shipwreck", and headed for Mérida, the largest town in the Yucatán. As was to be expected, the march was as uncomfortable as possible, winding for days through swamps, savannah infested with insects and verdant lagoons. While crouching in a canoe on the waters of Catazaja in the middle of a profusion of variously coloured birds of all species, Stephens realised and regretted that he was totally ignorant of the natural sciences. Catherwood was ill and when they finally arrived at the port of Laguna de Carmen on the gulf of Mexico after a dreadful crossing of the Terminos lagoon, Stephens was greatly relieved. But "Mr Catherwood" was not the type to declare himself beaten easily. He knew that Stephens was desperate to discover other lost cities and he declared himself ready to continue.

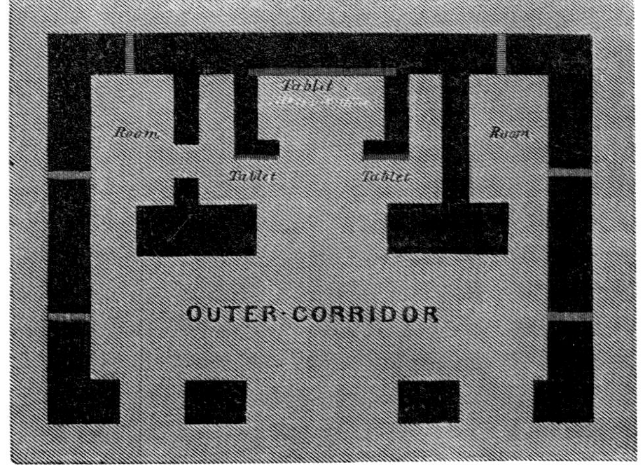

Page 146 – Spread stucco panel showing King Chan Bahlum in parade uniform, in the Temple of the Sun, Palenque.

Pages 146-147 – Prospect of the sanctuary inside the Temple of the Sun, Palenque.

Page 147 left – Prospect and plan of the Temple of the Sun, Palenque.

Page 147 right – Spread stucco panel showing the infernal God L, in the Temple of the Sun, Palenque.

From Carmen (where they left Pawling) they sailed as far as Sisal, the port of the lovely and large colonial city of Mérida, where they arrived on a broken down cart on the eve of Corpus Domini. Here Frederick literally collapsed devoured by malaria.

While in New York, Stephens had met a Hispano-American gentleman

Uxmal

Page 148 – A detail of the facade of the Governor's Palace, Uxmal.

Pages 148-149 – View of the ruins of Uxmal. To the right, the so-called "Pyramid of the Diviner", to the left the Quadrilateral of the Nuns.

by the name of Simón Peón who was a direct descendant of the Montejos, the true owners of the Yucatán from the 17th century on. He had invited Stephens to visit if he was passing through Mérida, adding that he was the owner of an entire ancient city, Uxmal, that would be of great interest. Stephens immediately went to find the principal residence of the Peón family but, unfortunately, Don Simón was at his hacienda in Uxmal about fifty miles off at the time. The two set off straightaway despite Catherwood's fever. Once they arrived at the hacienda, as Frederick was too weak to continue, the American left him in the care of their generous hosts and went off alone to visit the ghost city. He was met by a wonderful surprise because Uxmal, far from being suffocated by the exuberant tropical

Pages 162-163 – Partial view of the so-called "Quadrilateral of the Pigeon-loft", with its tall crests which have given the name to the building.

Page 163 – The facade of the House of the Turtles, which owes its name to the sculptures surmounting the mullioned frieze.

Palace was a real royal court in which audiences and important ceremonies were held, its true function is still unknown despite our knowledge that it was built on a precise astronomical orientation. From the central door, the Mayan astronomers were able to observe the rising of Venus each morning from behind a pyramid some miles away.

Uxmal contains many complexes and single buildings of extreme interest such as the Great Pyramid, the North Acropolis, the House of the Turtles, the Cemetery Group and the ball-court. Unfortunately, there is no inscription that can throw light on the reigning dynasties or historical events of the city. Little progress has been made in this field since Stephens, Catherwood and Cabot were camped on the site.

Helped by Cabot who was often willingly distracted by the sight of the brightly coloured birds that populated the ruins, Stephens and Catherwood cleaned and measured most of the buildings. The first achievement was an accurate site plan. Then Frederick started to draw the single buildings paying particular attention to the "Governor's Palace". His formidable experience told him that the construction techniques were the same as those used at Copán and Palenque although the decorations seemed different. They were therefore studying the remains of a people that at one time had extended its cultural influence over a vast territory. Stephens, meanwhile, had been studying the archives of nearby

UXMAL

villages and had discovered the Spanish transcription of a Mayan chronicle, the "Chilam Balam"; he too began to make connections between the various cities that they had explored up to that moment. All were built from stone on the basis of similar architectural rules and in each they had found inscriptions composed of the same symbols. For the American, the art and historical development of the cities they had visited made the Mayan civilisation, by then, an incontrovertible reality. Another point of interest was that during his journeys around Uxmal, Stephens had discovered a small Mayan pyramid fallen into rubble in a locality called El Laberinto near Maxcanú. Inside the pyramid he found a passage and he deduced that maybe other pyramids also had hidden rooms inside. This hypothesis was completely ignored by scholars but it was to be confirmed fifty years later by archaeologist Alberto Ruiz Lhuillier and other excavation programmes in the decades that followed.

Unfortunately, three weeks after their arrival, Stephens fell victim once more to malaria. It sent him into a fever and thoroughly weakened him. The priest of Ticúl, a nearby village where they were later to find more Mayan ruins, took Stephens into the monastery to take care of him but shortly afterwards both Cabot and an Indian servant, Albino, went down with the same illness. This time round, "Mr Catherwood" seemed to have been passed over and, while the poor priest was coping with three patients, he completed the entire documentation of the ruins of Uxmal alone. In the end though, he too succumbed to malarial fever.

Page 164 – The eastern side of the Pyramid of the Magician.

Pages 164-165 – The western side of the same building: the magnificent temple with entrance with serpent jaws is in the *Chenes* style, the top one in the *Puuc* style.

Kabah

When the three were ready to leave on January 1st 1842, the mules were loaded with chests filled with drawings, maps, original finds (including a carved wooden architrave found in the "Palace of the Governor") and plastercasts of the most representative sculptures and ornaments they had found. Their destination was Kabah, another large city that was once connected to Uxmal by an important road. The road was the means by which most commercial trade in the region had been carried out; a large and austere gateway with a corbelled vault marked its start.

Today this ancient Mayan centre has not been entirely excavated but is known for the Palace of the Masks, or Codz Pop which in the local language means "rolled mat". The entire facade of the building is decorated with large masks of Chac, the god with the long nose, which severely tested Catherwood's skill. To gain access to each room in the palace, it is necessary to climb up a step formed by the upturned nose of a mask which indeed resembles a rolled up mat. The other buildings in the ceremonial centre are

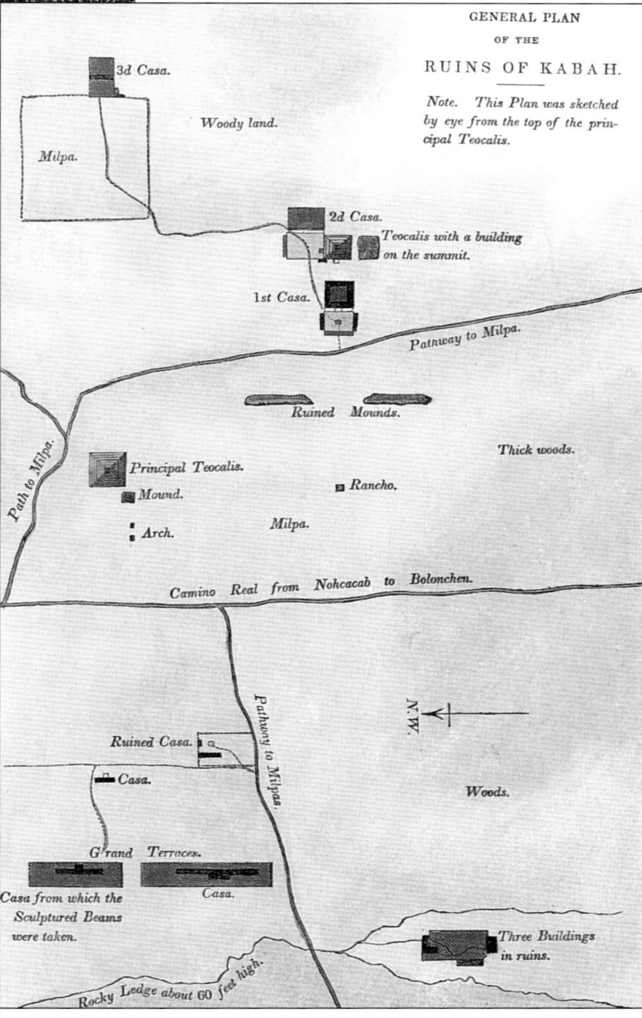

Pages 166-167 – The "Terzera Casa", one of Kabah's monumental buildings.

Page 167 bottom – Map of the site of Kabah.

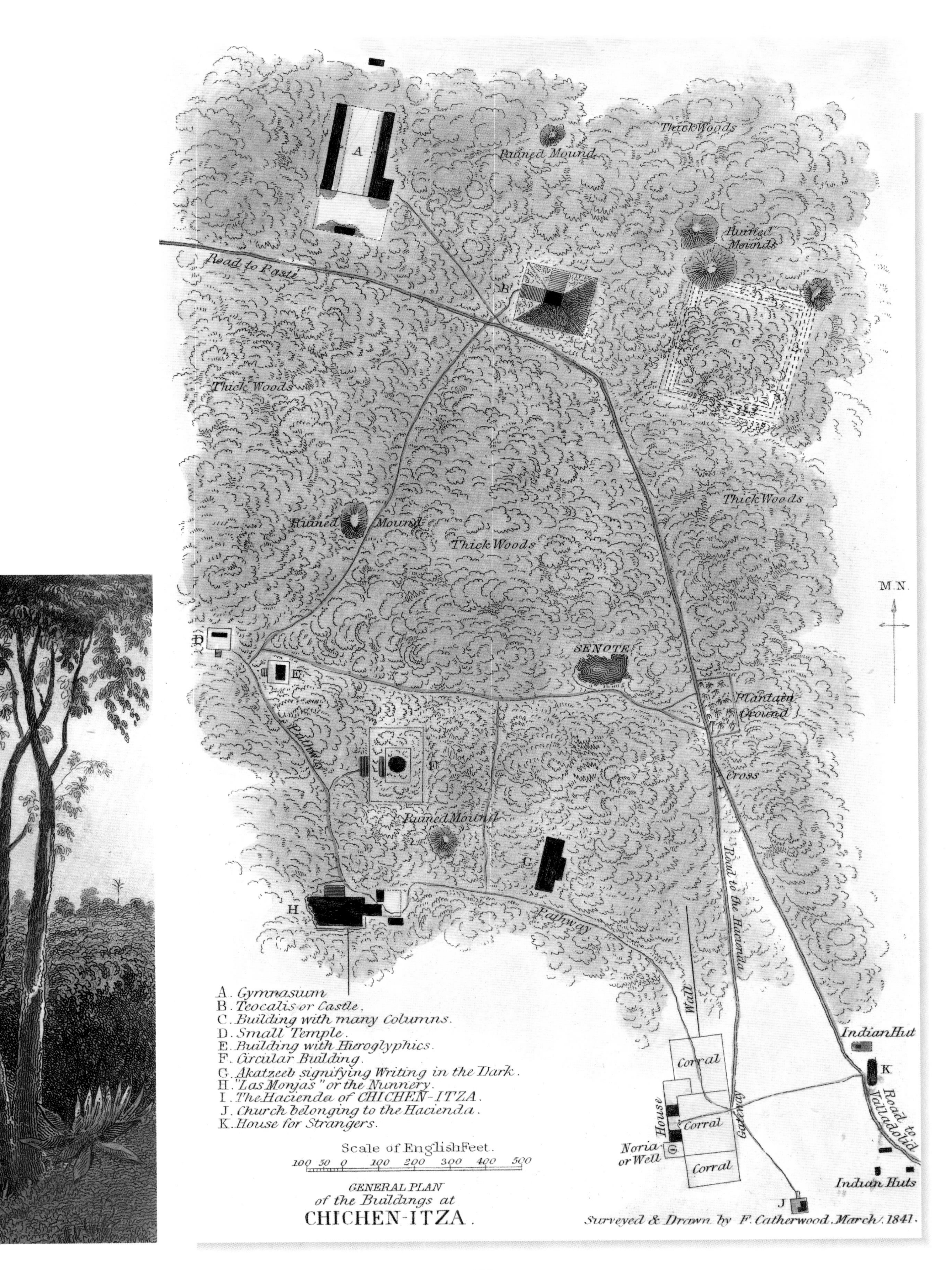

Thick Woods
Ruined Mound
Ruined Mounds
Road to Pisté
A
B
C
D
E
F
G
H
I
J
K
Thick Woods
Thick Woods
Ruined Mound
Thick Woods
M.N.
SENOTE
Plantain Ground
Pathway
Cross
Ruined Mound
Road to the Hacienda
Pathway
Wall
Corral
House
Corral
Noria or Well
Corral
Indian Hut
Road to Valladolid
Indian Huts
A. Gymnasium.
B. Teocalis or Castle.
C. Building with many Columns.
D. Small Temple.
E. Building with Hieroglyphics.
F. Circular Building.
G. Akatzeeb signifying Writing in the Dark.
H. "Las Monjas" or the Nunnery.
I. The Hacienda of CHICHEN-ITZA.
J. Church belonging to the Hacienda.
K. House for Strangers.
Scale of English Feet.
100 50 0 100 200 300 400 500
GENERAL PLAN
of the Buildings at
CHICHEN-ITZA.
Surveyed & Drawn by F. Catherwood. March 1841.

called Kukulkán. Around 1000 AD, Chichén Itzá had already been transformed into a vast urban centre endowed with monuments attesting to the syncretism of the Mayan culture of the Late Classic Period with that of the Toltecs. The sculpture and decorations show the influence of a strongly militarised elite compared to those in the lowland cities that had flourished in previous centuries. The warring ideology that was a feature of Mesoamerican civilisations in the centuries immediately preceding the Spanish conquest is extremely evident here. Both Catherwood and Stephens, by then experts, realized that some determining event had occurred at Chichén Itzá, although they observed the same peculiar traits of the Mayan cultures, including the hieroglyphic inscriptions. The influence of the Puuc style is only seen in some of the buildings in the southern area of the site, of which the most important are the Coloured House, the Church and the Nunnery. The facade of the latter is entirely covered with stone fret designs and masks connected with the ancient cults of Chac and the Terrestrial Monster. On the other hand, there is a number of severely styled buildings from the Toltec period: the Castle (a nine-stepped pyramid topped by a magnificent temple), the Caracol (a surprising cylindrical building used as an astronomical observatory), the largest

CHICHÉN ITZÁ

Page 182-183 top – The small building attached to the so-called "Nunnery": it is a splendid example of pre-Toltec *Puuc* style.

Page 183 – The "Iglesia", a magnificent structure adjacent to the previous building, dates from the Late Classical period.

Pages 182-183 bottom – The three-storeyed building known as the Nunnery.

church in New York; in it, Hawks said that he had met Stephens in London in 1836 at the time when the American was writing children's books for Harper Bros. and that it was Hawks himself who encouraged Stephens to take up a career in writing. The brilliant results of this encouragement still enthral readers around the world as the three books Incidents of Travel, *are obviously, the wish remained a dream. In September 1852 he was once more in California where he worked with alacrity on the Marysville railway project until April 1853. He then returned to London where he wanted at all costs to oversee the English reprint of* Incidents of Travel in Central America, *published in 1854 by Arthur Hall, Virtue & Co., to which which now covered Manhattan. Having departed from Liverpool with 385 passengers on board, the steamship SS Arctic was rammed by the French steamer Vesta off Newfoundland on 27 September 1854. The captain and many of the crew filled the few lifeboats and survived, but almost all the passengers were left to fend for themselves and they died miserably in the freezing waters of the*

periodically reprinted.

Catherwood was ignorant of his friend's death and wrote him a letter, today conserved at the Bankroft Library at the University of California, in which he explained his plans for the future. He told of his involvement in a mining company in California and of his ambitious desire to explore the ruins they had spoken of in Panama. He longed to undertake another expedition and make new lithographs to be added as an appendix to Stephens' books but, he added eight new engravings and the portrait of Stephens. Frederick also wrote a short introduction to the work in which he gave a short but accurate description of his friend. In September of the same year he made his umpteenth journey to New York to check in person how the Benecia-Marysville Railroad and Gold Hill companies were doing (Gold Hill was the mining company in which he had invested a good part of his savings) but he never saw the forest of buildings Atlantic. The news of the terrible disaster reached New York two weeks later with the list of the dead. In a mocking twist of fate, one name was missing – an oversight that smacks of incredible. Frederick's death was only verified after many days and at the insistence of Stephens' family.

"Mr Catherwood", architect, Egyptologist, artist, surveyor, painter, pioneer of Mesoamerican archaeology and railway builder, had passed away unnoticed, just as he had spent most of his extraordinary life.

Bibliography

- Claude François Baudez et Pierre Becquelin, *Les Mayas*, 1984.
- William Henry Bartlett, *Walks about the City and Environs of Jerusalem*, 1844.
- Frederick Catherwood, *Views of Ancient Monuments in Central America, Chiapas and Yucatan*, 1844.
- Brian M. Fagan, *The Rape of the Nile*, 1975.
- Paul Gendrop and Doris Heyden, *Mesoamerican Architecture*, 1989.
- Victor Wolfgang von Hagen, *Search for the Maya. The Story of Stephens and Catherwood*, 1973.
- Nicholas Reeves and Richard H. Wilkinson, *The Complete Valley of the Kings*, 1996.
- John Romer, *Valley of the Kings*, 1981.
- John Lloyd Stephens, *Incidents of Travel in Egypt, Arabia Petræa, and the Holy Land*, 1837.
- John Lloyd Stephens, *Incidents of Travel in Greece, Turkey, Russia, and Poland*, 1838.
- John Lloyd Stephens, *Incidents of Travel in Central America, Chiapas and Yucatan*, 1841.
- John Lloyd Stephens, *Incidents of Travel in Yucatan*, 1843.
- Henry Stierlin, *Mayan*, 1976.

The contract signed by Stephens and Catherwood on 9 September 1839 is conserved at the Bancroft Library, University of California, Berkeley together with numerous other papers belonging to Stephens and eighteen letters written to him by Catherwood from 1839 on (Collection Number: BANC MSS-Z-Z-116).

Illustration Credits

Private Collection / Archivio White Star: Pages 12, 13, 14, 15, 16-17, 18 top, 18-19, 19 centre, 19 bottom, 26, 30, 31, 33 bottom, 35, 36, 37.
Frederick Catherwood, Views of Ancient Monuments in Central America, Chiapas and Yucatan, London 1844, Archivio White Star: Pages 1, 2, 3-6, 7, 8-9, 10-11, 44, 45, 46-47, 49, 50-51, 53, 54-55, 57, 58-59, 60-61, 62-63, 64-65, 66-67, 68-69, 71, 73, 74-75, 77, 78-79, 80-81, 82-83, 85, 86-87, 89, 90-91, 93, 94-95, 97, 98-99, 100-101, 102-103, 104-105, 106-107.
John L. Stephens, Incidents of Travel in Central America, Chiapas and Yucatan, London 1841, Archivio White Star: Pages 108, 109, 110, 111, 112, 113, 114, 115, 116, 117, 118, 119, 120, 121, 122, 123, 124, 125, 126, 127, 128, 129, 130, 131, 132, 133, 134, 135, 136, 137, 138, 139, 140, 141, 142, 143, 144, 145, 146, 147, 148, 149, 150, 151.
John L. Stephens, Incidents of Travel in Yucatan London 1843, Archivio White Star: Pages 152, 153, 154, 155, 156, 157, 158, 159, 160, 161, 162, 163, 164, 165, 166, 167, 168, 169, 170, 171, 172, 173, 174, 175, 176, 177, 178, 179, 180, 181, 182, 183, 184, 185, 186, 187, 188, 189, 190, 191, 192, 193, 194, 195, 196, 197, 198, 199.
Robert Hay, Views in Cairo, London 1840, Archivio White Star: Pages 22 bottom left, 23 top.
Agenzia Luisa Ricciarini: Page 17 centre.
AKG Photo: Pages 38, 39.
Ashmolean Museum, Oxford, The Bridgeman Art Library: Page 16 top.
William Henry Bartlett, Walks about the City and Environs of Jerusalem, London 1844, Archivio White Star: Pagg. 28, 29.
Courtesy Bancroft Library, University of California: Page 43 left.
Christie's Images: Pages 32-33.
Civica Raccolta A. Bertarelli, Castello Sforzesco, Milano: Page 17 bottom.
E.T. Archive: Page 16 left.
Fototeca Storica Nazionale, Milan: Page 17 top right.
Giraudon, Musee des Beaux Art Nantes, The Bridgeman Art Library: Page 21 right.
Mary Evans Pictures Library, London: Pages 17 top left, 21 top.
Societe de Geographie, Paris: Page 40 left.
Sotheby's Library: Page 19 top.
Stapleton Collection, The Bridgeman Art Library: Page 20 top.
The Bridgeman Art Library, London: Pages 40-41, 41 top, 42.
Courtesy the British Library: Page 27.
The Fine Art Society, London, The Bridgeman Art Library: Pages 20-21.
Victoria & Albert Museum, London: Pages 22-23, 24-25.

The maps and old prints were hand colored by Old Church Galleries, London.